Biblical Portrait of the Woman

(60 days scriptures for a Praying Woman)

Joy Mowete

**Biblical Portrait of the Woman
(60 days scriptures for a Praying Woman)**
Copyright © 2018 by Kochi Exclusive Solutions Ltd.

Cover Design by Kochi Exclusive Solutions Ltd.
Bluecrest Mall, Suite 34, Abijo Lagos, Nigeria.
+234 1 2915255,+234 7061058860
kmowete@yahoo.com

Scriptures taken from the New King James Version. Copyright
© 1982 by Thomas Nelson, Inc. used by permission. All rights
reserved.

International Standard Book Number:
ISBN 978-978-962-219-1

Visit the author at her website: www.declarehisword.com

Dedication

I dedicate this book to all the women all over the
world.
To all the women who are hungry –
may the Lord feed you with His Word.
To all the women who are thirsty –
may the Lord fill you with His Holy Spirit.
To all the women who feel empty –
may the Lord fill you to overflowing with His
Presence.
To all the women who are weak –
may the Lord empower you with His Strength.
To all the women who are sorrowful –
may the Lord Comfort you.
To all the women who are confused –
may the Light of Jesus Christ shine into your body,
soul & spirit.
To all the women who are lonely or feel unloved –
may the Love of Jesus Christ surround you.
And to all the women who are strong and running
the race –
may the Lord strengthen you and give you grace to
finish well.

ACKNOWLEDGMENTS

I thank you, Almighty God for calling me to pray, to worship and to write. I am grateful and I give you all the glory.

My darling and my publisher, Kenneth Mowete. I love you.

I wish to extend my sincere acknowledgment and appreciation to my Pastor, Pastor Siju Iluyomade and The Handmaidens of The Redeemed Christian Church of God (RCCG), City of David Parish for the Women in Leadership Series, Theme: LEADING WOMEN, LEADING CHANGE 2016. It was a one day conference of women coming together, to talk on how to improve our lives, to be vessels unto honour for the kingdom of God and to help build our nation. At the end of the meeting, as I sat down at the back, looking at the women in attendance, it came to my spirit – "will it not be nice to write prayers for the woman"? Then I answered (in my spirit) it will be wonderful!

That was how the Biblical Portrait of the Woman (60 days scriptures for a Praying Woman) was conceived and born!

Thank you Ma, for bringing us together. God bless you.

It is written

John 14:23
**Jesus answered and said to him
"If anyone loves Me, he will keep My word;
and My Father will love him, and
We will come to him and make Our home
with him.**

Psalm 119:162
**I rejoice at thy word,
as one that findeth great spoil.**

THE JOURNEY

A female child is born

From a female child she becomes a beautiful little baby girl

From a baby girl she becomes a promising teenage girl

From a teenager she becomes a young adult – full of life

From a young adult she becomes a young woman - strong & ready

From a young woman she becomes a woman

Thank you Lord for being with me through all the different stages

Thank you Lord that I am a woman

Introduction

Biblical Portrait of the Woman

(60 days scriptures for a Praying Woman) is written to:

- Help the woman know what the Bible says concerning her.
- Help her to pray using the Word of God.
- Help her to build an intimate relationship with her Creator.
- Help her to develop her prayer life.

I recommend you start each day by inviting the Holy Spirit, our Helper and Teacher to help you pray and teach you the Word of God. As you read the Word for the day, STUDY IT and MEDITATE ON IT, I believe God will use it to bless, guide and order your steps. God bless you as you read and pray in His word.

Day 1

Exodus 2:2
"So the woman conceived and bore a son. And when she saw that he was a beautiful child, she hid him three months."

Thank you LORD that I am a woman.
I am blessed.
I am fruitful spiritually in Jesus name.
I am fruitful naturally in Jesus name.
The children the Lord has given to me are beautiful.
They are beautiful children before God and before men.
My family and I are hidden in the LORD.
We belong to you, Almighty God forever and ever in Jesus Name.

Day 2

Psalm 113:9

"He grants the barren woman a home, like a joyful mother of children."

Thank you LORD that I am a woman.
The LORD has given me a home.
He has honoured me in my home.
He has destroyed everything that
represents barrenness in my life.
I am fruitful in every area of my life.
The LORD has made me a joyful mother of
children.
The joy of the LORD is continually in my
home.
The shout of hallelujah will always be in my
home in Jesus Name.

Day 3

Proverbs 5:18-20

"Let your fountain be blessed, and rejoice with the wife of your youth. As a loving deer and a graceful doe, let her breasts satisfy you at all times, and always be enraptured with her love. For why should you, my son, be enraptured by an immoral woman, and be embraced in the arms of a seductress?"

Thank you LORD that I am a woman.
The fountain of my husband is blessed.
My husband will continue to rejoice with me the wife of his youth.
I am as lovely as an angel. I am as beautiful as a rose. My breasts satisfy my husband at all times. He is enraptured with my love.
He is always surrounded with my love.
My husband, the son of the Most High God, will never find delight with an immoral woman. He will never be found in the embrace of the strange woman in Jesus Name.

Day 4

Proverbs 18:22
"He who finds a wife finds a good thing, and obtains favor from the LORD."

Thank you LORD that I am a woman.
My husband has found me.
I am his wife. I am a good thing.
I am joy, I am Ayo, I am Anwuli, I am faithful, I am beautiful, I am lovely, I am patient, I am meek, I am humble, I am a child of God, I am redeemed through the blood of Jesus Christ, I am kind, I am compassionate, I am a worker in the vineyard of God.
In every area of my husband's life, he finds favor.
I declare, the favor of God is upon him. I declare, the favor of man is upon him in Jesus Name.

1: Ayo, Anwuli means joy

Day 5

Proverbs 11:16

"A gracious woman retains honor but ruthless men retain riches."

Thank you LORD that I am a woman.

I am a gracious woman.

I am a pleasant woman.

I am well-favoured, precious and kind.

I have excellent manners.

I exhibit courtesy and politeness.

I bring honour to my husband.

I bring respect to my household in Jesus Name.

Day 6

Proverbs 12:4
**"An excellent wife is the crown of her husband,
but she who causes shame is like rottenness in his
bones."**

Thank you LORD that I am a woman.

I am an excellent wife.

I am a virtuous woman.

I am a righteous woman.

I am the crown of my husband.

I am his joy and pride.

Father, by your mercy, do not allow me to
bring shame to my husband.

Help me LORD never to cause him dishonor.

My husband is happy and pleased with me
in Jesus Name.

Day 7

Proverbs 14:1
"The wise woman builds her house, but the foolish pulls it down with her hands."

Thank you LORD that I am a woman.

I am a wise woman.

I am filled with the wisdom of God.

My home is built and rooted in the word of God.

My Father, by your grace, do not let me do anything that will bring destruction to my home.

LORD, do not let me do anything that will bring destruction to my life.

My life is beautiful and pleasing to God in Jesus Name.

Day 8

Proverbs 31:10-12

"Who can find a virtuous wife? For her worth is far above rubies. The heart of her husband safely trusts her; so he will have no lack of gain. She does him good and not evil all the days of her life."

Thank you LORD that I am a woman.
Father, by your grace, I am a virtuous wife.
By your grace LORD, I am an intelligent and a capable wife.My worth is far above rubies.
The heart of my husband safely trusts me.
My husband will not lack anything good spiritually and naturally.
As long as I have life within me, I will be good to my husband.
I will not cause him harm. He is blessed to have me as his wife in Jesus Name.

Day 9

Proverbs 31:30-31
"Charm is deceitful and beauty is passing, but a woman who fears the LORD, she shall be praised. Give her of the fruit of her hands, and let her own works praise her in the gates."

Thank you LORD that I am a woman.
Charm can mislead and beauty can disappear but a woman who honours and serves the LORD should be praised.
I am a woman who honours and serves the LORD with all her heart.
LORD, please, let me be a woman after your own heart.
Bless the works of my hands.
Cause them to be profitable.
Father, let my good works bring you glory and honour in Jesus Name.

Day 10

Isaiah 49:15

"Can a woman forget her nursing child, and not have compassion on the son of her womb? Surely they may forget, yet I will not forget you. See, I have inscribed you on the palms of My hands; your walls are continually before Me."

Thank you LORD that I am a woman.
Thank you Almighty God for being my Father.
According to your word, you will never forget me.
I am your daughter.
I am redeemed through the blood of your Son, Jesus Christ.
You have written my name on the palms of your hands.
My walls, O LORD are continually before you. I am yours forever in Jesus Name.

Day 11

Matthew 9:22

"But Jesus turned around, and when He saw her He said, "Be of good cheer, daughter; your faith has made you well." And the woman was made well from that hour."

Thank you LORD that I am a woman.
Just as the woman in the book of Matthew 9:22 got the attention of Jesus Christ; I declare and decree into my life that today, I receive divine assistance from heaven in Jesus name.
I am of good cheer.
I am joyful.
I am the daughter of the Most High God.
My faith is in God.
From this hour, I am made well. I am delivered from every evil. I am restored. I am healed. I am whole in Jesus Name.

Day 12

Matthew 26:7

"A woman came to Him having an alabaster flask of very costly fragrant oil, and she poured it on His head as He sat at the table."

Thank you LORD that I am a woman.
Just as this woman in the book of Matthew 26:7 played her role in the life of Jesus Christ, My Father, I ask for grace to fulfill every plan and purpose you have for me.
LORD, the wisdom, knowledge and understanding I need to do your will, please, grant to me.
Help me LORD to love you with all my heart, with all my mind and with all my soul in Jesus Name.

Day 13

Mark 5:27-29

"When she heard about Jesus, she came behind Him in the crowd and touched His garment. For she said, "If only I may touch His clothes, I shall be made well." Immediately the fountain of her blood was dried up, and she felt in her body that she was healed of the affliction."

Thank you LORD that I am a woman. Lord Jesus Christ, you are my Lord and Savior. You are my Healer.
As I call your name Jesus Christ, I command everything that represents sickness, disease and afflictions in my life to dash to the ground and be destroyed in Jesus name.
By the punishment you suffered Jesus Christ, I am healed. By the blows you received, I am made whole. No more sickness, no more disease and no more afflictions in my life in Jesus Name.

Day 14

Luke 13:11-13
"And behold, there was a woman who had a spirit of infirmity eighteen years, and was bent over and could in no way raise herself up. But when Jesus saw her, He called her to Him and said to her, "Woman, you are loosed from your infirmity." And He laid His hands on her and immediately she was made straight and glorified God."

Thank you LORD that I am a woman.
Thank you for the finished work of the cross.
Just as the woman in the book of Luke 13:11-13 got the attention of Jesus Christ and was set free from the spirit of infirmity, I declare into my life, from today, I get the attention of heaven. I command every long standing issue affecting my life to receive solution from heaven right now in Jesus name. In the mighty name Jesus Christ, I am healed and I am whole. Father, thank you, for your power to heal and cure me is available and is working in Jesus Name.

Day 15

Acts 9:36

"At Joppa there was a certain disciple named Tabitha, which is translated Dorcas. This woman was full of good works and charitable deeds which she did."

Thank you LORD that I am a woman.
I am a disciple of my Lord Jesus Christ.
Father, by your grace, my name is written in the book of life.
I am full of good works.
I am a worthy worker in God's vineyard.
I am a vessel unto honour in His hand.
The grace to help out is upon me.
I am a witness of my Lord Jesus Christ in Jesus Name.

Day 16

Acts 16:14-15

"Now a certain woman named Lydia heard us. She was a seller of purple from the city of Thyatira, who worshiped God. The Lord opened her heart to heed the things spoken by Paul. And when she and her household were baptized, she begged us, saying, "If you have judged me to be faithful to the Lord, come to my house and stay." So she persuaded us."

Thank you LORD that I am a woman.
Father, I lift up the works of my hands unto you, help me LORD to be successful in my place of work.
Help me LORD to be a woman who worships you with all her heart, mind and soul.
Open my heart LORD to heed to your word. Help me to be a faithful and fruitful worker in your vineyard. Holy Spirit, help me to be sensitive and obedient to all your instructions in Jesus Name.

Day 17

Genesis 2:24
"Therefore a man shall leave his father and mother and be joined to his wife and they shall become one flesh."

Thank you LORD that I am a woman.
Father, thank you for the gift of family.
Thank you LORD for the family I came from.
Thank you LORD for my immediate family.
Thank you for the man you have given to me as my husband.
Thank you for making me his beautiful wife.
My husband has left his father and mother and has become one with me, his wife.
Father, bless us, guide us, protect us, help us and order all our steps.
Father, let our home be your home forever and ever in Jesus Name.

Day 18

1 Samuel 1:19-20
"Then they rose early in the morning and worshiped before the LORD, and returned and came to their house at Ramah. And Elkanah knew Hannah his wife and the LORD remembered her. So it came to pass in the process of time that Hannah conceived and bore a son and called his name Samuel, saying, "Because I have asked for him from the LORD."

Thank you LORD that I am a woman.
My family and I receive grace to arise, early every morning to praise the LORD.
My husband loves me.
Today, the LORD will remember me for good. All God's promises I have been pregnant with, I call them forth into manifestation right now in Jesus name.
All my children are gifts from you, LORD.
I commit all of them into your holy hand in Jesus Name.

Day 19

Ruth 4:13-14

"So Boaz took Ruth and she became his wife and when he went in to her, the LORD gave her conception and she bore a son. Then the women said to Naomi, "Blessed be the LORD, who has not left you this day without a close relative and may his name be famous in Israel!"

Thank you LORD that I am a woman.
Father, thank you for the life of my husband.
Thank you for making us husband and wife
Thank you for making us one in you.
Thank you LORD for giving me conception.
Thank you for making me mother of children.
I declare and decree that my family and I will praise and bless the name of the Lord forever. I declare and decree that my family and I will make Jesus Christ famous in Jesus Name.

Day 20

Psalm 128:3
"Your wife shall be like a fruitful vine in the very heart of your house, your children like olive plants all around your table."

Thank you LORD that I am a woman.
Thank you LORD for making me a wife.
I am fruitful and I bring forth abundantly.
I am like a fruitful vine in the very heart of my home.
Thank you LORD for the gift of my children.
My children are like olive plants all around my table.
My family and I are fruitful and faithful in the kingdom of God in Jesus Name.

Day 21

Proverbs 19:14
"Houses and riches are an inheritance from fathers, but a prudent wife is from the LORD."

Thank you LORD that I am a woman.
My Father in heaven, with a heart full of joy, I thank you today for making me the wife of my husband.
I am a prudent, prosperous and successful wife.
I am a gift from God to my husband.
I bring joy and honour to him.
I am wise and sensible.
I am filled with the wisdom of God in Jesus Name.

Day 22

Isaiah 54:1

"Sing, O barren, you who have not borne! Break forth into singing and cry aloud, you who have not labored with child! For more are the children of the desolate than the children of the married woman." says the LORD."

Thank you LORD that I am a woman.
The LORD has given me a new song.
I will praise and worship God all the days of my life.
The Almighty God has destroyed everything that represents barrenness in my life.
I declare and decree in the name of Jesus Christ, I am fruitful.
Today, I break forth into singing and praising God.
My God has been faithful and merciful to me.
I am blessed with beautiful and wonderful children.
My family and I will forever be useful in the kingdom of God in Jesus Name.

Day 23

1 Peter 3:1
"Wives, likewise, be submissive to your own husbands, that even if some do not obey the word, they, without a word, may be won by the conduct of their wives. When they observe your chaste conduct accompanied by fear."

Thank you LORD that I am a woman.
I am submissive to my husband.
I am humble and loving.
My life brings glory to God.
My ways of life draw men to the kingdom of God.
I have excellent manners.
I am obedient to my husband.
By my godly conduct, I bring him honour and respect in Jesus Name.

Day 24

Ephesians 5:22-23

"Wives, submit to your own husbands, as to the Lord. For the husband is head of the wife, as also Christ is head of the church and He is the Savior of the body."

Thank you LORD that I am a woman.

I am submissive to my husband as to the Lord.

As Christ is the Head of the church, that is how my husband is my head.

Things and characters that will make me not be submissive to my Lord Jesus Christ, blood of Jesus purge them out.

Things and characters that will make me not be submissive to my husband, precious blood of the Lamb wipe them out in Jesus Name.

Day 25

Ephesians 5: 25, 28

"Husbands, love your wives, just as Christ also loved the church and gave Himself for her." "So husbands ought to love their own wives as their own bodies, he who loves his wife loves himself."

Thank you LORD that I am a woman.
My husband is a gift from God to me.
I have the love, support and attention of my husband.
As Christ loved the church and gave Himself for her that is how my husband loves and cherishes me.
As my husband loves his own body, that is how he loves me.
I plead the blood of Jesus Christ over our love and over our love for you, LORD.
Father, thank you for the grace to love.
Please, keep us rooted forever in your unending love in Jesus Name.

Day 26

John 8:10-11

"When Jesus had raised Himself up and saw no one but the woman, He said to her, "Woman, where are those accusers of yours? Has no one condemned you?" She said, "No one, Lord." And Jesus said to her, "Neither do I condemn you; go and sin no more."

Thank you LORD that I am a woman. Thank you Lord Jesus Christ for the finished work of the cross. Thank you for your precious blood that cleanses me from every sin. I declare and decree Jesus Christ; you are my Lord and Savior.

I am not living under condemnation.

My Lord Jesus Christ did not condemn me. He came to give me life and life in abundance. I have the abundant life of Jesus Christ. Sin has no dominion over me. I triumph over sin and iniquity in Jesus Name.

Day 27

John 19:25

"Now there stood by the cross of Jesus His mother, and His mother's sister, Mary the wife of Clopas, and Mary Magdalene."

Thank you LORD that I am a woman.
I am redeemed through the blood of Jesus Christ.
My Lord Jesus Christ, thank you for saving me.
As Mary, the mother of Jesus and her sisters stood by the cross of Jesus, My Father, I ask for the grace to always take my stand by you. LORD, I pray that nothing will separate me from you.
My Father, please, keep me rooted in you that no matter what happens to me, I will be yours forever.
I declare before the whole world today, that I belong totally to Jesus Christ in Jesus Name.

Day 28

Proverbs 21:9
**"Better to dwell in a corner of a housetop, than in
a house shared with a contentious woman."**

Thank you LORD that I am a woman.

I am excellent woman.

My husband dwells quietly and peacefully
with me.

I am not a nagging woman.

I am not a quarrelsome woman.

I am not a fault finding woman.

Christ is the Rock in which my home is built.

I am a loving and peaceful woman in Jesus
Name.

Day 29

Proverbs 21:19
"Better to dwell in the wilderness, than with a contentious and angry woman."

Thank you LORD that I am a woman.
I am a godly woman.
I am not a nagging wife
I am not a complaining wife
I am patient and tolerant.
I am loving and forgiving.
I dwell happily with my husband
The glory of God is in my home in Jesus Name.

Day 30

Judges 13:3-4

"And the Angel of the LORD appeared to the woman and said to her, "Indeed now, you are barren and have borne no children, but you shall conceive and bear a son. Now therefore, please be careful not to drink wine or similar drink, and not to eat anything unclean."

Thank you LORD that I am a woman.
In the name of Jesus Christ, I will fulfill every God's plan and purpose for my life.
Every God's plan for me that I have been pregnant with, in the mighty name of Jesus Christ, I begin to bring forth now.
Father, by your grace, help me to live a healthy life style.
Precious Blood of Jesus Christ, cleanse everything in my life that does not glorify God. May my life style, both private and public bring glory to God in Jesus Name.

Day 31

Ruth 3:1

"Then Naomi her mother-in-law said to her, "My daughter, shall I not seek security for you, that it may be well with you?"

Thank you LORD that I am a woman.
Father, thank you for the gift of family.
Father, thank you for my home.
I declare and decree, it is well with me in my matrimonial home.
It is well with all the members of my household.
It is well with all that concerns me.
The LORD God Almighty is our Protector.
He watches over us day and night.
No evil will come near our dwelling in Jesus Name.

Day 32

Ruth 3:11

"And now, my daughter, do not fear. I will do for you all that you request, for all the people of my town know that you are a virtuous woman."

Thank you LORD that I am a woman.
My Father, fill me with your Spirit of
Wisdom, Knowledge and Understanding.
Holy Spirit, please, help me that my heart
will always be in tune with the heart of my
heavenly Father.
As Ruth was known as a virtuous woman in
town, in the name of Jesus Christ, I declare,
I am a woman of fine character.
I am a living witness of my Lord and Savior,
Jesus Christ, in Jesus Name.

Day 33

John 11:25-27

"Jesus said to her, "I am the resurrection and the life, He who believes in Me, though he may die, he shall live, and whoever lives and believes in Me shall never die. Do you believe this?" She said to Him, "Yes, Lord, I believe that You are the Christ, the Son of God, who is to come into the world."

Thank you LORD that I am a woman.
Lord Jesus Christ, I believe in you.
You are the resurrection and the life.
I have an abundant life in you.
I shall not die.
When I close my eyes to this earth,
I will open them to eternity.
Lord, you are the Messiah, the Son of God,
Who is to come into the world in Jesus
Name.

Day 34

Luke 10:40-42

"But Martha was distracted with much serving and she approached Him and said, "Lord, do You not care that my sister has left me to serve alone? Therefore tell her to help me." And Jesus answered and said to her, "Martha, Martha, you are worried and troubled about many things. But one thing is needed, and Mary has chosen that good part, which will not be taken away from her.""

Thank you LORD that I am a woman.
Lord, give me the grace to be heavenly focused in all that I do.
Help me LORD, in my spiritual life, not to be distracted.
Help me LORD, in my natural life, not to be distracted.
Help me LORD, to be calm in every situation.
Holy Spirit, please, guide me into all things.
I have chosen the good part, I have given my life to Christ, He is my Lord and Savior in Jesus Name.

Day 35

1 Kings 17:9
"Arise, go to Zarephath, which belongs to Sidon, and dwell there. See, I have commanded a widow there to provide for you."

Thank you LORD that I am a woman.
Thank you LORD for your abundant love for me.
You are my Provider; you always make way for me.
Father, I ask for your grace to always obey your instructions, both those I understand and those I do not understand.
I arise out of everything holding me down and become who the LORD has made me to be.
I receive help from heaven.
I receive help from my divine helpers.
Use me LORD to be a divine helper to someone in Jesus Name.

Day 36

1 Kings 17:24

"Then the woman said to Elijah, "Now by this I know that you are a man of God, and that the word of the LORD in your mouth is the truth."

Thank you LORD that I am a woman.
Father, please, give me the wisdom to know what to do at any given time.
Help me LORD, to daily read and study your word.
Help me LORD, to know the truth.
Help me LORD to be in the right fellowship.
My Father, help me to be your true representative on earth.
Help me Father to be heavenly focused in all that concerns me in Jesus Name.

Day 37

2 Kings 4:8
"Now it happened one day that Elisha went to Shunem, where there was a notable woman, and she persuaded him to eat some food. So it was, as often as he passed by, he would turn in there to eat some food."

Thank you LORD that I am a woman.
I declare and decree, I am a notable woman of God.
I am a vessel of honour in the hand of God.
As this notable woman helped Elisha,
Father, today, I surrender all to you, fill me afresh with your Holy Spirit and use me for your Kingdom.
Use me LORD, for my family,
Use me LORD, for the church,
Use me LORD, for my nation,
Use me LORD, for the nations of the world in Jesus Name.

Day 38

2 Kings 4:17
"But the woman conceived, and bore a son when the appointed time had come, of which Elisha had told her."

Thank you LORD that I am a woman.
I am a fruitful woman.
I bear fruits spiritually and naturally.
The ideas and plans God has for me,
I call them forth into manifestation in Jesus name.
God's plans and purpose for my life will not be destroyed, at the right season, they shall all manifest.
All that the LORD has promised me in His word, by prophecy, both private and public shall all come to pass in Jesus Name.

Day 39

2 Kings 8:6
"And when the king asked the woman, she told him. So the king appointed a certain officer for her, saying, "Restore all that was hers, and all the proceeds of the field from the day that she left the land until now."

Thank you LORD that I am a woman.
Thank you for all the good times.
Thank you for all the difficult times.
Thank you for being with me always.
Thank you LORD for my guardian angels.
Angels of restoration, right now in the name of Jesus Christ, restore to me all God's promises for my life.
I call forth into full manifestation all God's promises for my life right from the day of conception to this very day in Jesus Name.

Day 40

Ecclesiastes 7:26
"And I find more bitter than death the woman whose heart is snares and nets, whose hands are fetters. He who pleases God shall escape from her, but the sinner shall be trapped by her."

Thank you LORD that I am a woman.
I am a woman who loves the LORD.
I am a woman who loves and cherishes her husband.
I am not a woman who is like a trap for her husband.
I am not a woman whose love for her husband will catch him like a net.
I am not a woman whose arms round her husband will hold him like a chain.
My husband's ways are pleasing to the LORD.
I am a godly woman. I am a woman whose love for her husband is pure in Jesus Name.

Day 41

Revelation 12:16
"But the earth helped the woman, and the earth opened its mouth and swallowed up the flood which the dragon had spewed out of his mouth."

Thank you LORD that I am a woman.
My help comes from the LORD who made heaven and earth.
In the name of Jesus Christ, I command the earth to help me.
The sun will not hurt me during the day
The moon will not kill me at night.
In the name of Jesus Christ, I command the earth to open its mouth and swallow up the flood of evil that has come out of the mouth of the enemy against my life in Jesus Name.

Day 42

Revelation 12:17

"And the dragon was enraged with the woman, and he went to make war with the rest of her offspring, who keep the commandments of God and have the testimony of Jesus Christ."

Thank you LORD that I am a woman.
Father, I thank you for your divine protection over me.
From every war the enemy is waging against me and my family, Father, deliver us.
From every war the enemy has planned to wage against my offspring, Father, deliver them.
Help us LORD, to be obedient to all your commands.
I declare that my family and I have the testimony of Jesus Christ, in Jesus Name.

Day 43

Luke 1:30
**"Then the angel said to her, "Do not be afraid,
Mary, for you have found favor with God."**

Thank you LORD that I am a woman.
I am not afraid.
God has not given me the spirit of fear.
He has given me the spirit of love, of power
and of sound mind.
By the power of the Holy Spirit of God,
I can do all He has created me to do.
I have found favor with God.
The Almighty God is with me.
I am not alone in Jesus Name.

Day 44

Luke 1:38

"Then Mary said, "Behold the maidservant of the Lord! Let it be to me according to your word." And the angel departed from her."

Thank you LORD that I am a woman.
I am the handmaid of the LORD.
Father, according to your plans and purpose for my life, let it be done.
Angel Gabriel, as you brought good news to Mary, today, bring good news to me.
Angels of God, you are ministering spirits sent forth to minister to me, today, minister to me in all that concerns me in Jesus Name.

Day 45

Luke 2:36-37

"Now there was one, Anna, a prophetess, the daughter of Phanuel, of the tribe of Asher. She was of a great age, and had lived with a husband seven years from her virginity, and this woman was a widow of about eighty-four years, who did not depart from the temple, but served God with fastings and prayers night and day."

Thank you LORD that I am a woman. Thank you LORD for the gift of eternal life through your beloved Son, Jesus Christ. According to your word in the book of Luke 2:36-37, Anna served you with fasting and prayer night and day, my Father, I ask for the grace to serve you with all my heart. Father, give me the grace to wait upon you. Help me LORD to be a dedicated worker in your vine yard. Help me LORD to be your witness in Jesus Name.

Day 46

Esther 5: 2

"So it was, when the king saw Queen Esther standing in the court, that she found favor in his sight, and the king held out to Esther the golden scepter that was in his hand. Then Esther went near and touched the top of the scepter."

Thank you LORD that I am a woman. As Esther found favor in the sight of the king, my Father, help me to always find favor in your sight and in the sight of men. As the king held out the golden scepter to Esther and she touched the top, my Father, you sent your only begotten Son, Jesus Christ to the world to redeem me and to give me abundant and eternal life; I receive Him as my Lord and Savior. Through the blood of Jesus Christ, I am redeemed, I am cleansed, I am purified, I am justified, I am sanctified in Jesus Name.

Day 47

Genesis 2:23-24
"And Adam said: This is now bone of my bones and flesh of my flesh; She shall be called Woman, Because she was taken out of Man.Therefore a man shall leave his father and mother and be joined to his wife, and they shall become one flesh."

Thank you LORD that I am a woman.
My Father, thank you for the gift of marriage.
I rebuke and curse the root of same sex marriage. Same sex marriage, in the name of Jesus Christ, you are not allowed in my family, you are not allowed in the church of Christ, you are not allowed in my nation in Jesus Name. God's plan for marriage will stand.
My husband has left his father and mother and is joined to me, his wife. We have become one flesh, praise the LORD, Hallelujah. LORD, please, keep us united always as one in Jesus Name.

Day 48

Genesis 1:28
**"Then God blessed them, and God said to them,
"Be fruitful and multiply; fill the earth and subdue
it; have dominion over the fish of the sea, over
the birds of the air, and over every living thing
that moves on the earth."**

Thank you LORD that I am a woman.
The blessings of God make me rich and
there are no sorrows to them.
I am fruitful spiritually and naturally.
I multiply spiritually and naturally.
I fill the earth spiritually and naturally
I subdue the earth spiritually and naturally.
I have dominion over the fish of the sea, I
have dominion over the birds of the air, I
have dominion over every living thing that
moves on the earth in Jesus Name.

Day 49

Genesis 21:1-2
"And the LORD visited Sarah as He had said, and the LORD did for Sarah as He had spoken. For Sarah conceived and bore Abraham a son in his old age, at the set time of which God had spoken to him."

Thank you LORD that I am a woman.
Thank you LORD, for you are a covenant keeping God.
LORD, as you visited Sarah, today, visit me.
LORD, you did for Sarah as you had spoken, today, remember me and do for me all that you had spoken concerning me.
I am fruitful in my marriage.
I am the mother of my husband's children.
At the set time, all that God had spoken about me shall manifest in Jesus Name.

Day 50

Genesis 30:22

"Then God remembered Rachel, and God listened to her and opened her womb."

Thank you LORD that I am a woman.
Thank you LORD for you are a God who keeps records and who remembers.
According to your word in Genesis 30:22, you remembered Rachel.
My Father, today remember me for good.
LORD, you listened to Rachel.
Today, listen to me and help me.
You opened Rachel's womb.
LORD, today, open my womb spiritually and naturally and cause me to be abundantly fruitful in all that concerns me in Jesus Name.

Day 51

Esther 4:16

"Go, gather all the Jews who are present in Shushan, and fast for me; neither eat nor drink for three days, night or day. My maids and I will fast likewise. And so I will go to the king, which is against the law; and if I perish, I perish!"

Thank you LORD that I am a woman.
Father, give me the grace to be courageous.
LORD, give me the grace to always pray, read the word, worship, fast and wait on you.
Spirit of the Living God, guide me in all things.
Father, help me not to faint, not to give up and not to be weary.
Help me to be strong till the end.
Father, help me not to deny you.
Even in a very difficult situation, Father, help me to declare that Jesus Christ is my Lord and Savior in Jesus Name.

Day 52

Judges 4:4-5

"Now Deborah, a prophetess, the wife of Lapidoth, was judging Israel at that time. And she would sit under the palm tree of Deborah between Ramah and Bethel in the mountains of Ephraim. And the children of Israel came up to her for judgment."

Thank you LORD that I am a woman.
Deborah was a prophetess and a judge in Israel, my Father, help me to be a reliable and dependable worker in your vineyard.
Help me LORD to fulfill the plans and purpose you have for my life.
Father, fill me with your wisdom.
Help me LORD, to be a soul winner.
Help me LORD to abound in good works in Jesus Name.

Day 53

Matthew 15:28
"Then Jesus answered and said to her, "O woman, great is your faith! Let it be to you as you desire." And her daughter was healed from that very hour."

Thank you LORD that I am a woman.
In the name of Jesus Christ, I declare and decree, I am a woman of great faith.
All my hope is in the LORD.
All my trust is in Him.
In Jesus name, all I want from the LORD will be done for me.
Jesus Christ, you are my healer.
I am healed of all afflictions, all diseases, all oppressions and infirmities.
I am whole in Jesus Name.

Day 54

Matthew 25:1-2
"Then the kingdom of heaven shall be likened to ten virgins who took their lamps and went out to meet the bridegroom. Now five of them were wise, and five were foolish."

Thank you LORD that I am a woman.
My Father, please help me to be wise.
Help me LORD to know what to do at any given situation.
I rebuke the spirit of foolishness.
I am filled with the Holy Spirit of God.
I have the spirit of wisdom.
In all my daily activities, I am led by the Holy Spirit in Jesus Name.

Day 55

Matthew 28:5-7

"But the angel answered and said to the women, "Do not be afraid, for I know that you seek Jesus who was crucified. He is not here, for He is risen, as "He said. Come, see the place where the Lord lay. "And go quickly and tell His disciples that "He is risen from the dead, and indeed He is going before you into Galilee; there you will see Him. Behold, I have told you.""

Thank you LORD that I am a woman.
Jesus Christ, I believe you are the Son of God.
 I believe you are the Way, the Truth and the Life.
You are alive. You have risen from the grave. You are seated at the right hand of God. I am seated together in the heavenly places with you.
LORD, help me to seek you.
LORD, help me to be your true disciple in Jesus Name.

Day 56

Mark 1:30-31

"But Simon's wife's mother lay sick with a fever, and they told Him about her at once. So He came and took her up, and immediately the fever left her. And she served them."

Thank you LORD that I am a woman.
Lord, thank you for your power to heal and cure me is available and is working.
My Lord, I lift up my life into your hands.
I command every area that is sick to receive your healing touch right now in Jesus Name.
I command everything that represents the spirit of fever to leave right now in Jesus Name.
By your stripes Lord, I am healed and I am whole.
As you have healed me Lord, use me as a vessel for healing, in Jesus Name.

Day 57

Mark 3:33-35

"But He looked around in a circle at those who sat about Him, and said, "Here are My mother and My brothers!" For whoever does the will of God is My brother and My sister and mother."

Thank you LORD that I am a woman.
Almighty God, you are my Father.
Jesus Christ, you are my Lord and Savior.
Holy Spirit, you are my Teacher and Helper.
Holy Spirit, please help me to know the will of God.
Father, I ask for grace to do your will always.
Lord Jesus Christ, I declare, I am yours forever in Jesus Name.

Day 58

Luke 1:24-25

"Now after those days his wife Elizabeth conceived; and she hid herself five months, saying, "Thus the Lord has dealt with me, in the days when He looked on me, to take away my reproach among people."

Thank you LORD that I am a woman.
Thank you LORD for making me a mother.
Thank you LORD for the gift of my children.
I pray for all those looking unto you for the fruits of the womb. Father, as you cause Elizabeth to conceive, help them to conceive and bear children.
LORD, you dealt well with Elizabeth, My Father, by your mercy, remember them and bless them. I command everything that represents reproaches in our lives to dash to the ground and be destroyed now in Jesus Name.

Day 59

Luke 1:57-58

"Now Elizabeth's full time came for her to be delivered, and she brought forth a son. When her neighbors and relatives heard how the Lord had shown great mercy to her, they rejoiced with her."

Thank you LORD that I am a woman.
Thank you for all the children you have given to me.
Thank you LORD for safe deliveries.
I lift up all the pregnant women into your hands.
As Elizabeth brought forth safely, that is how all of them will bring forth safely in Jesus name.
LORD, today, do something beautiful, something great, something marvellous that will showcase your Glory and your awesome Presence in my life in Jesus Name.

Day 60

Luke 7:13-15

"When the Lord saw her, He had compassion on her and said to her, "Do not weep". Then He came and touched the open coffin, and those who carried him stood still. And He said, "Young man, I say to you, arise." So he who was dead sat up and began to speak. And He presented him to his mother."

Thank you LORD that I am a woman.
Lord Jesus Christ, I know you, you are the Resurrection and the Life.
You had compassion on this woman, Lord, by your mercy, have compassion on me.
I shall not weep over my children.
In Jesus name, I command every good thing in my life that is dead, to arise and receive the divine touch of Jesus Christ right now and be alive.

OTHER BOOKS BY THE AUTHOR

I know who I am in Christ Jesus
(Biblical Confessions for 365 Days)
God's Divine Provision
(31 Days Scriptural Declarations for Provision)
God's Healing Promises
(31 Days of Healing Declarations)

Coming soon:
Total Deliverance
(31 Days Scriptures for Total Deliverance)
God's Inner Peace
(90 Days Scriptural Declarations of God's covenant of peace with me)
Living Under God's Covering
(90 days Biblical Declarations for Protection)
Exercising Divine Authority
(90 days scriptural declarations for Healing, Provision & Deliverance)

Have you been blessed with our book(s)? Do you have any suggestion or comment? We would love to hear from you. Please contact us:
joykent@declarehisword.com

NOTE:

NOTE: